Date: **Sign:**

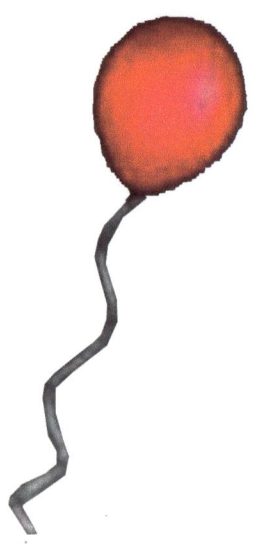

...now go live your dreams...

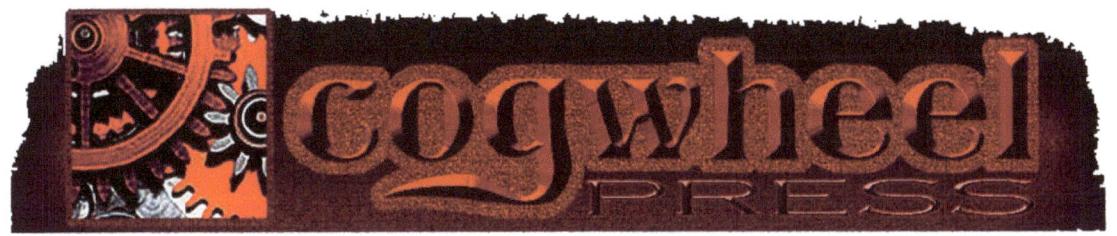

ISBN-13: 978-1507551622
ISBN-10: 1507551622

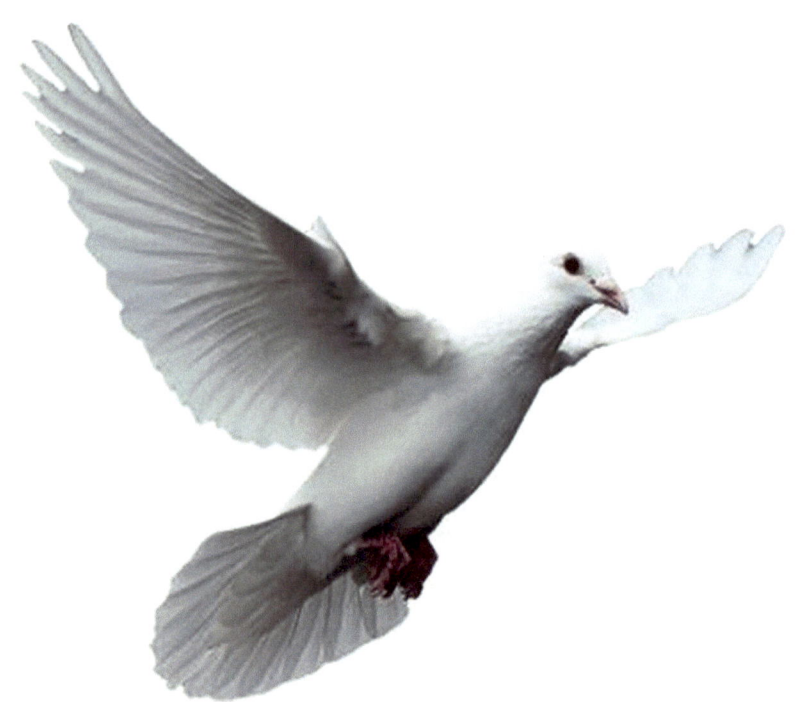

The inspiration for this book...

Please accept our invitation to set aside all differences with your fellow man and come together for a memorial and a celebration.

Following the events of terror in Paris, France in January 2015, the world mourned the loss of many lives to hate crimes. For the citizens of The United States of America, we were reminded of 9/11. Many things changed for our nation following that historical day. The people of France are some of our oldest allies. To forget them in their time of loss would be to deny the cause for which we fought the Revolutionary War.

In response to the violence that shook the world, we have a very special message for our youth and lovers of liberty. A new children's picture-book, filled with the wonder and imagination of childhood... a witness to free will!

Little Red Balloon is a symbol of a desire for life and liberty; a reminder to liberate others when they have been downtrodden. May this book motivate you to be a beacon of light in a dark world; an advocate for free will... and may you be the one who cuts the string when someone is tied down.

This book is a hymn to freedom, a collaboration between Desiree Finkbeiner, American best-selling author, and Jean-Luc Adde, award-winning French photographer, to honor the friendship of two nations, the United States and France.

On every page we find whimsical images of human beings with animal heads, they look at us with mischief, hilarious and sometimes strange, set in a faerie-like imaginary world; through the pages, a little red balloon travels, twirls, plays with the reader... a symbol of freedom with a hint of nostalgia.

Desiree Finkbeiner & Jean-Luc Adde

"Where liberty dwells,
there is my country."

Benjamin Franklin

Little Red Balloon
petit ballon rouge

A little red balloon

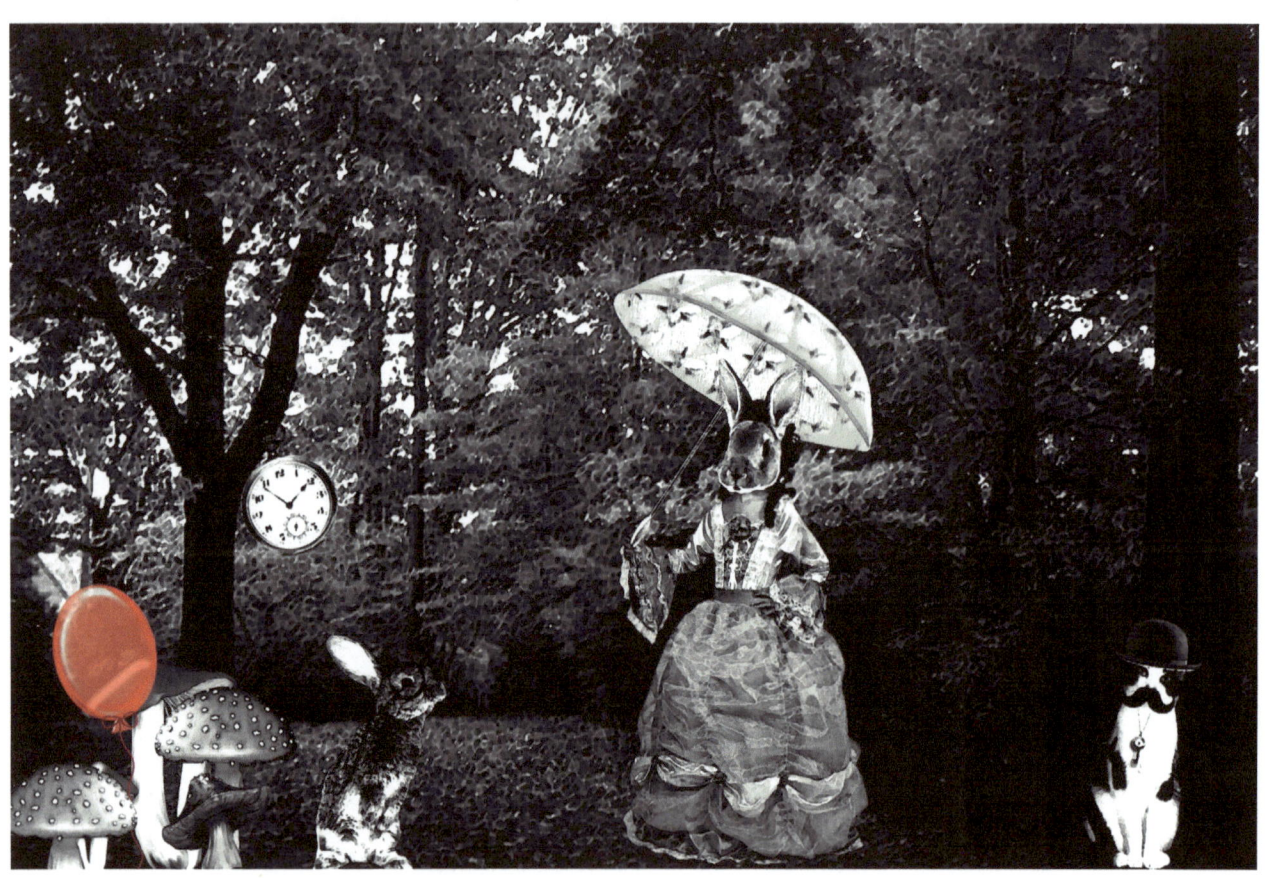

was tied onto a string.

But how he longed to soar the skies,

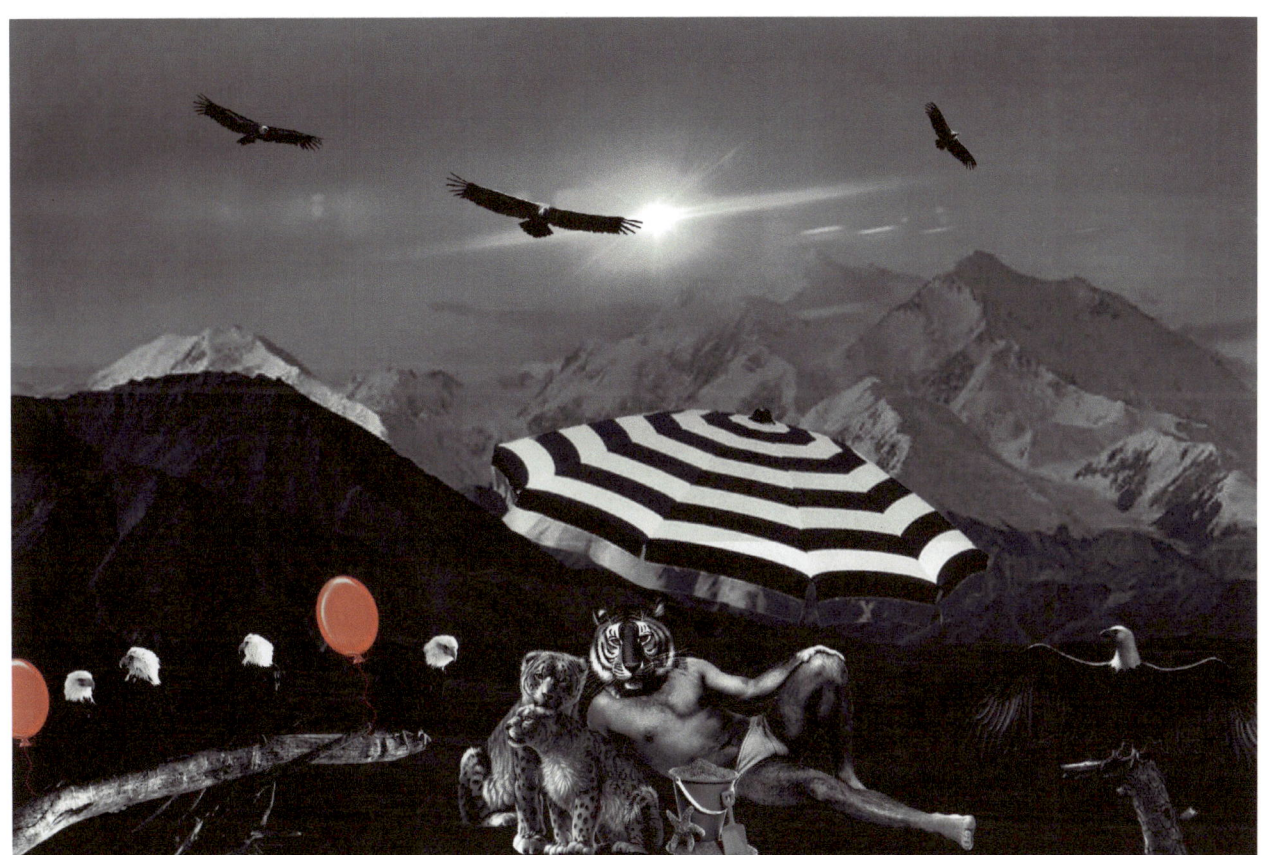

like birds do on their wings.

He felt trapped, to be tied up,

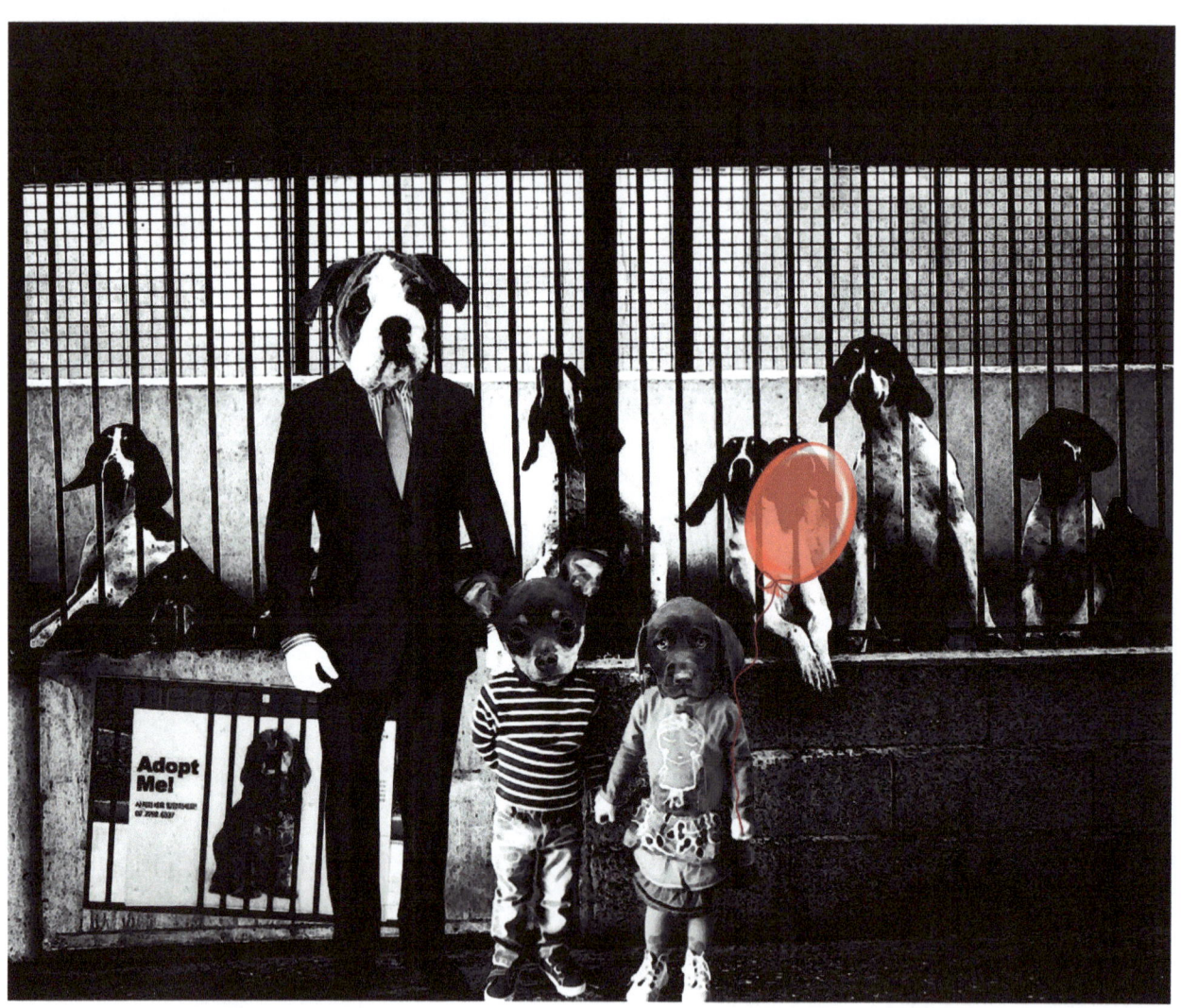

always fastened down.

In the hands of other folks,

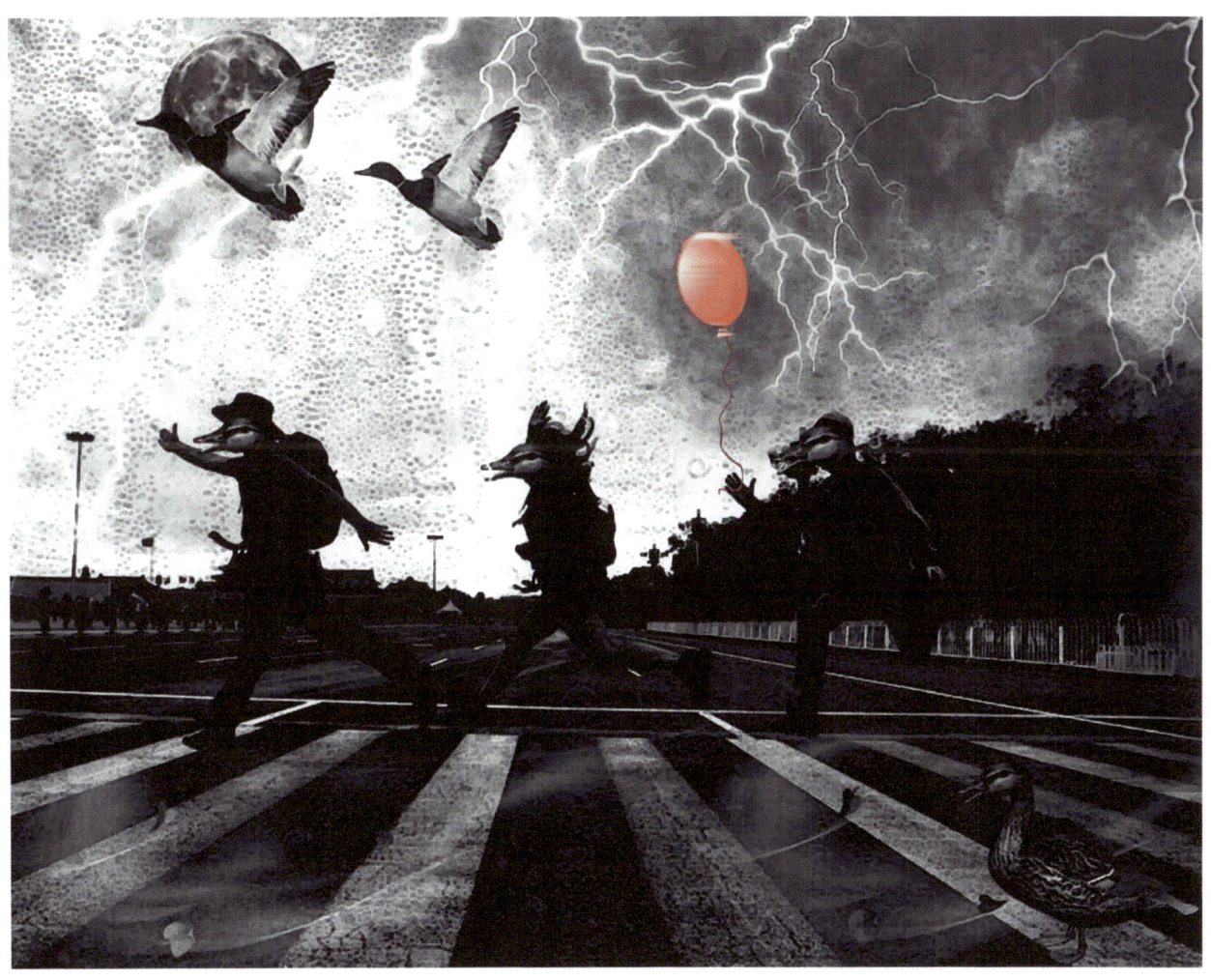

he passed around the towns.
Though he saw some lights and streets,

some barns

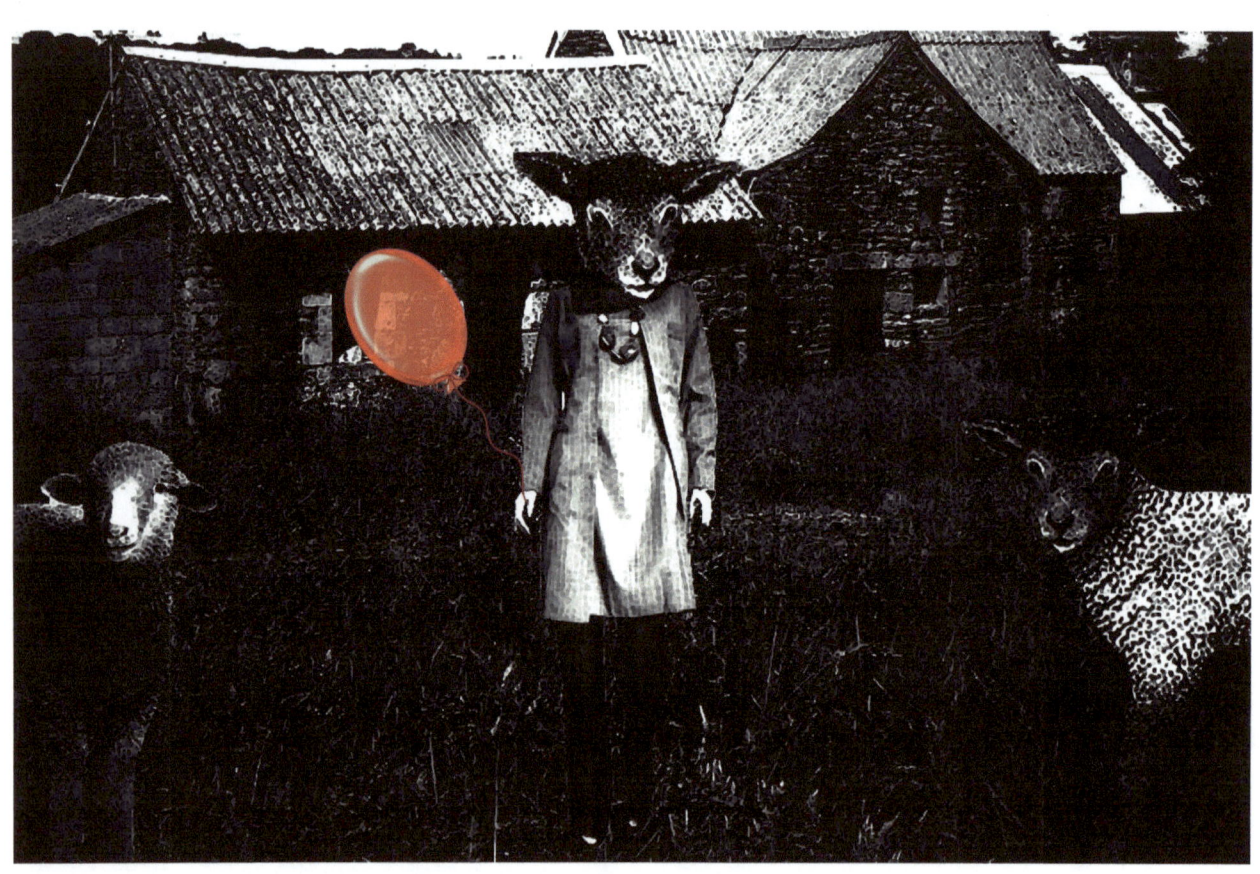

and stables too,

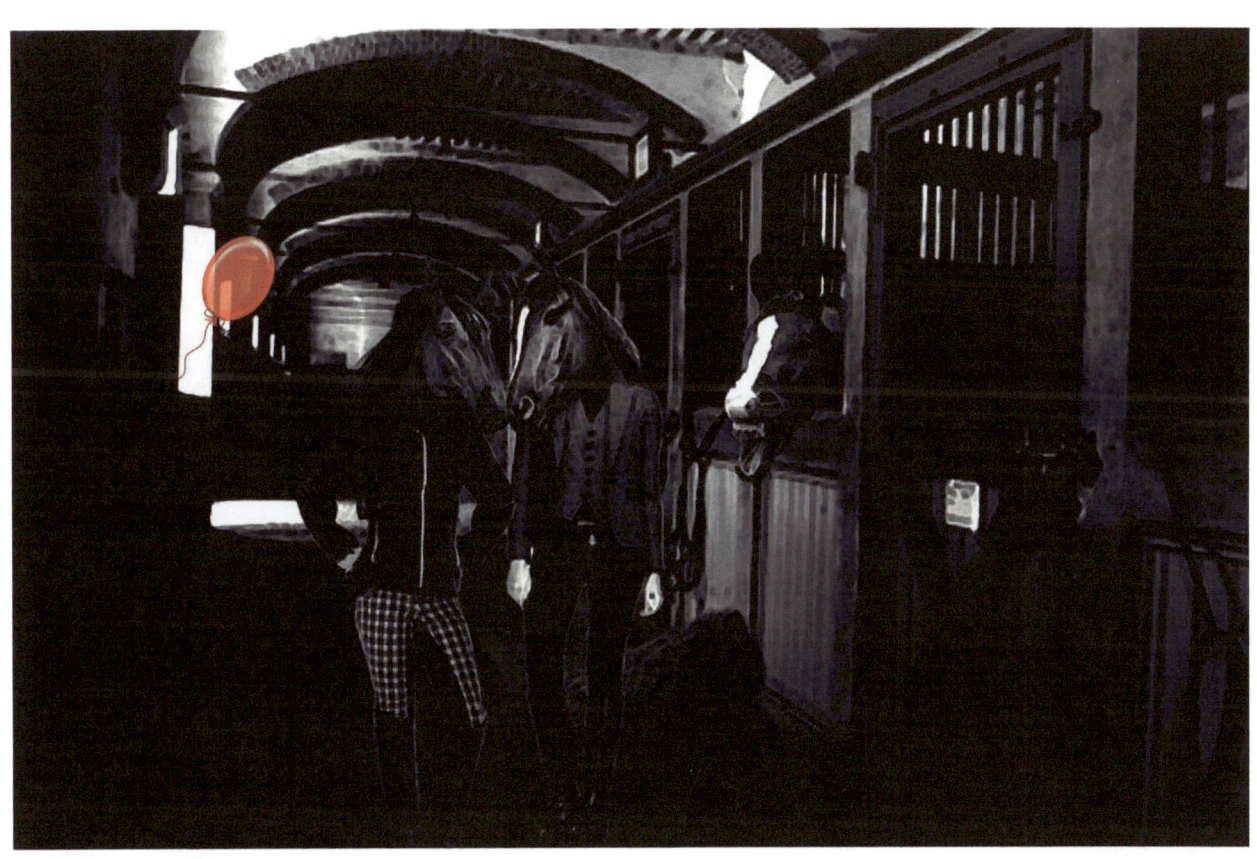

nothing could erase his dream

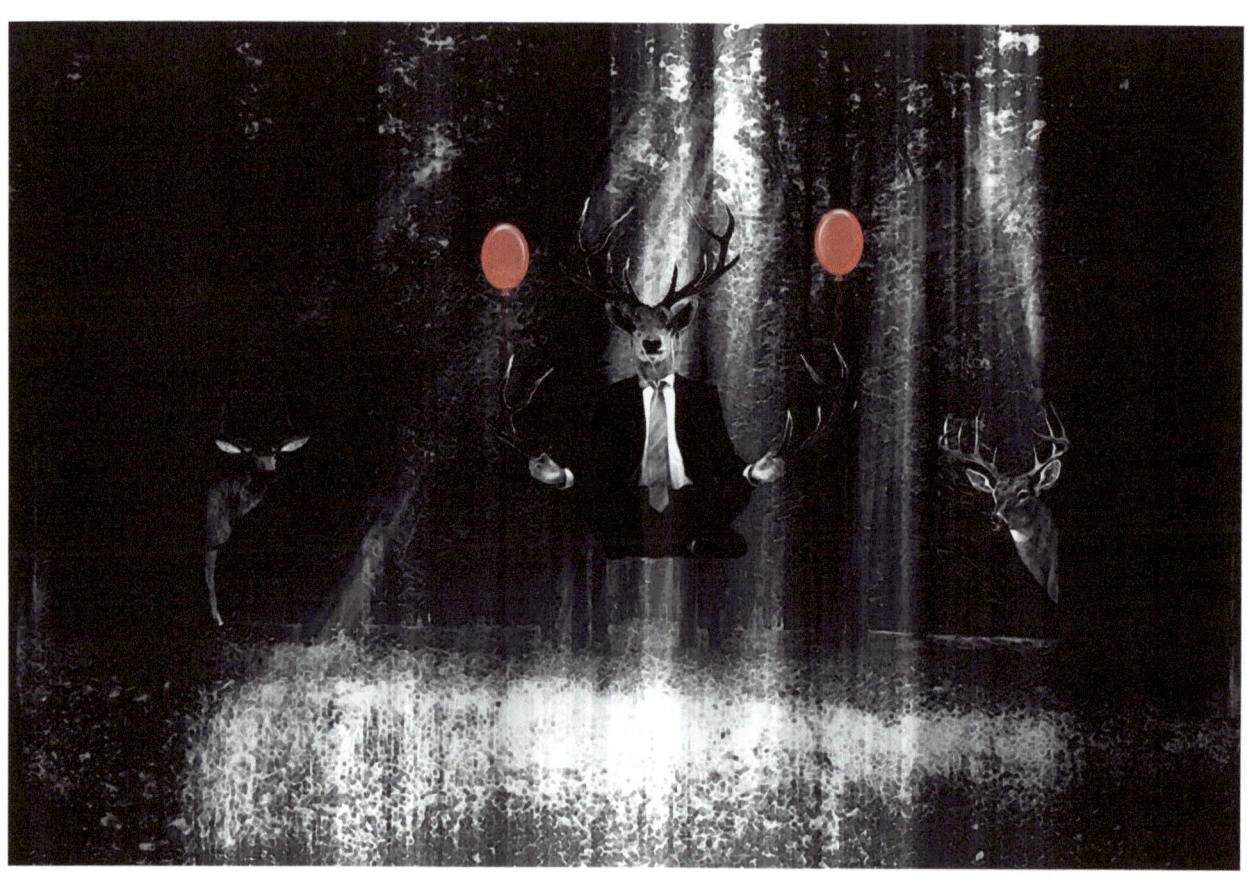

of having his own view.

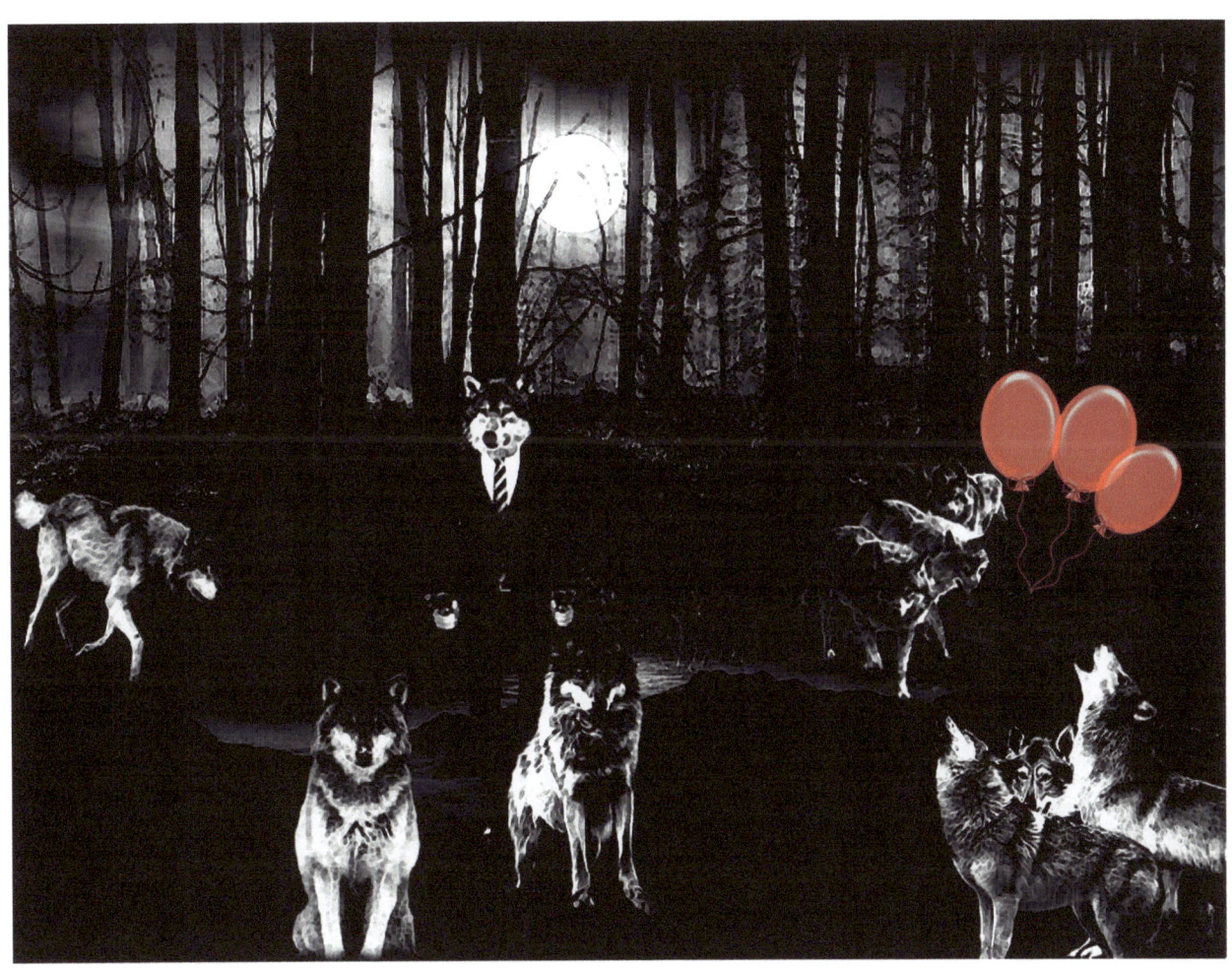

A little girl noticed how he drooped,

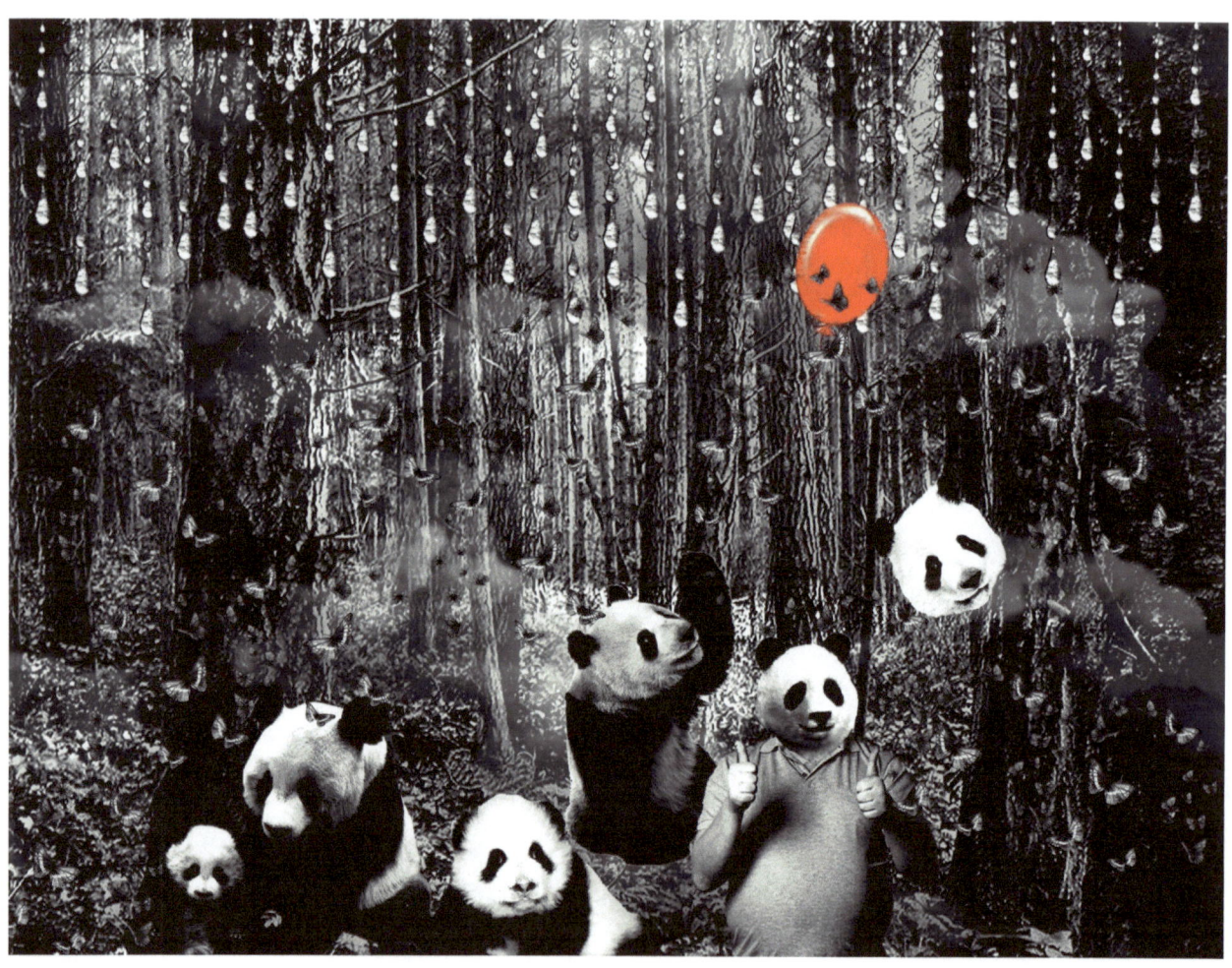

and asked him why he frowned.

"Because, you see, I wish to be free

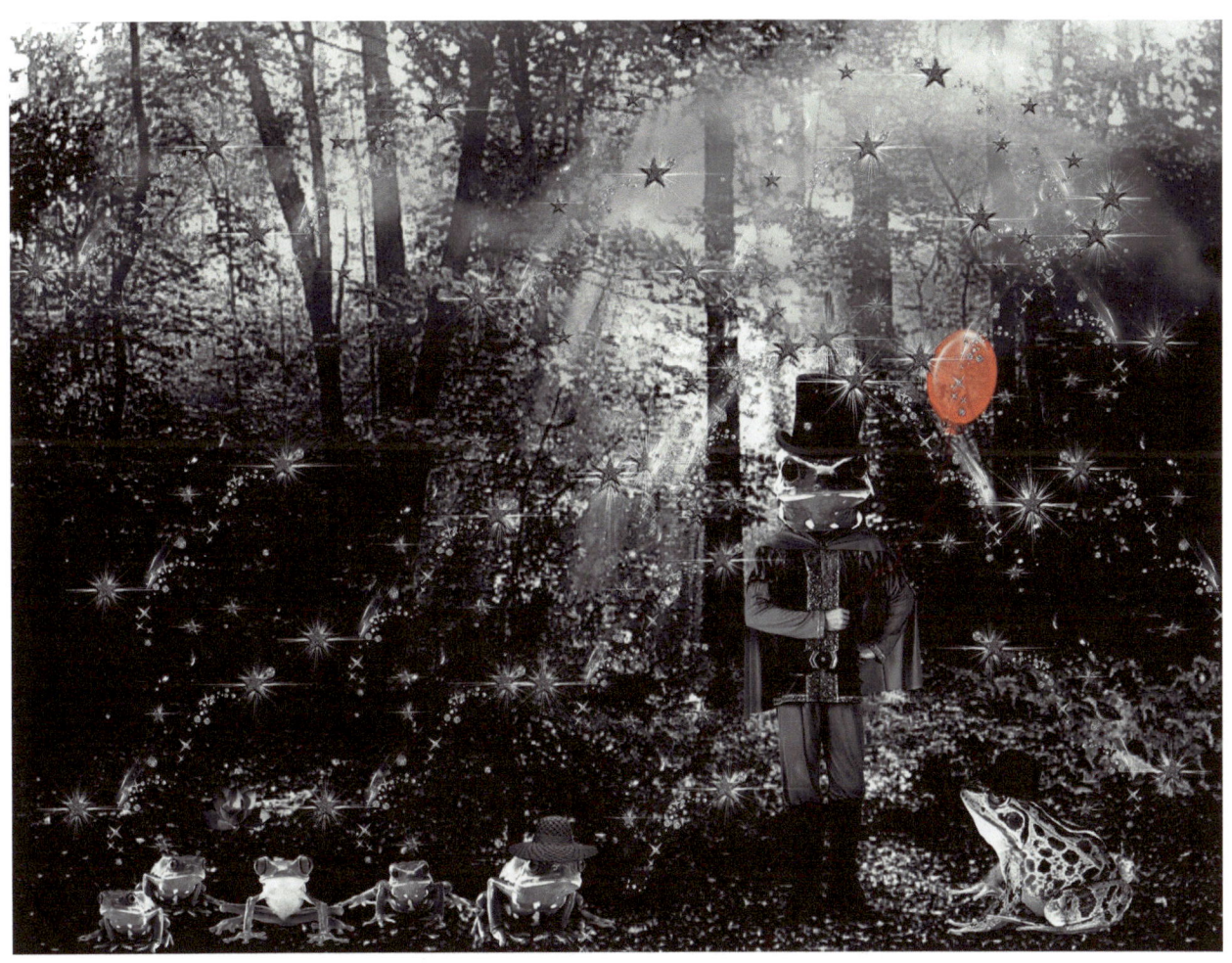

but here I am tied down."

"Then let me help you on your way!"

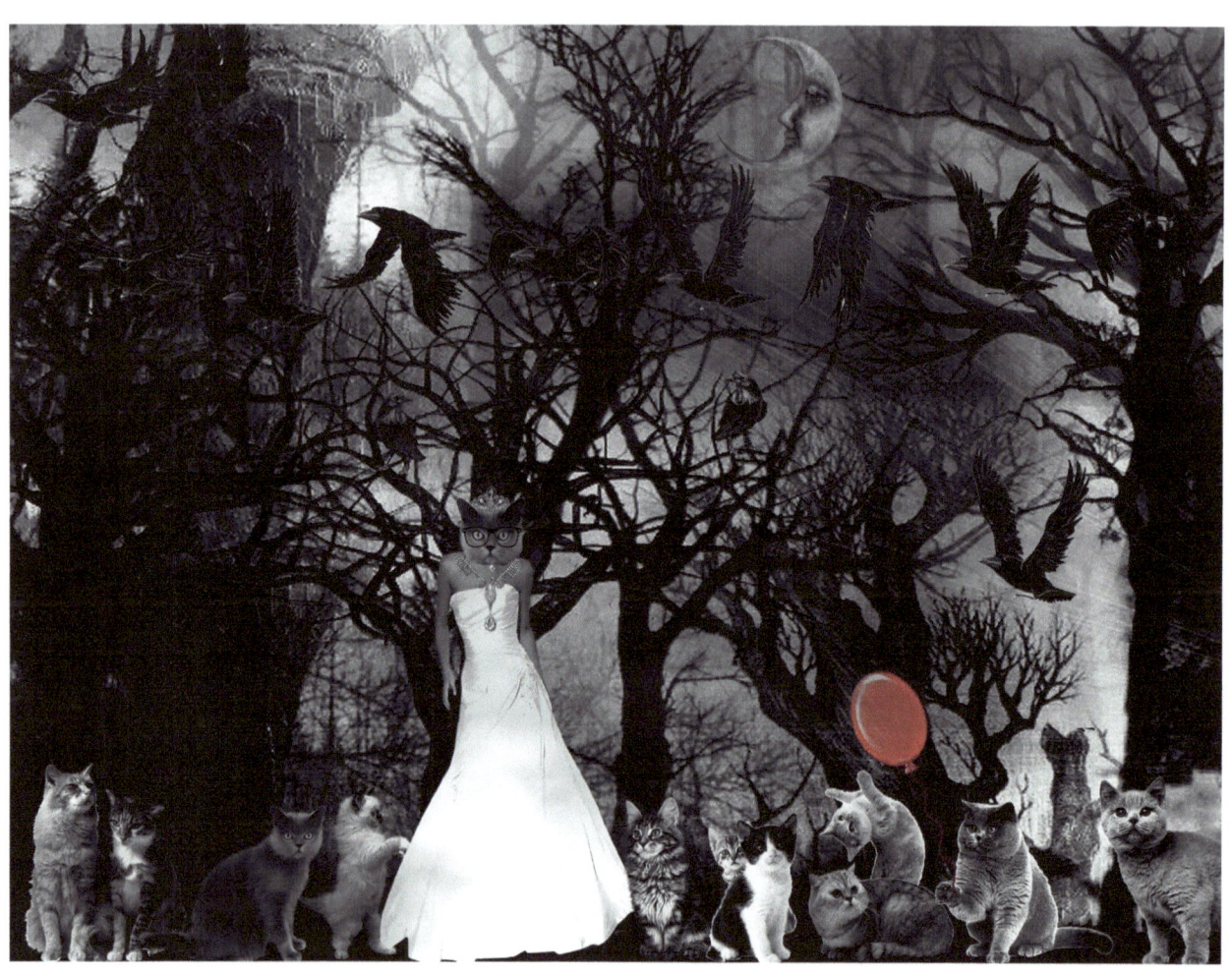

And she cut away his string...

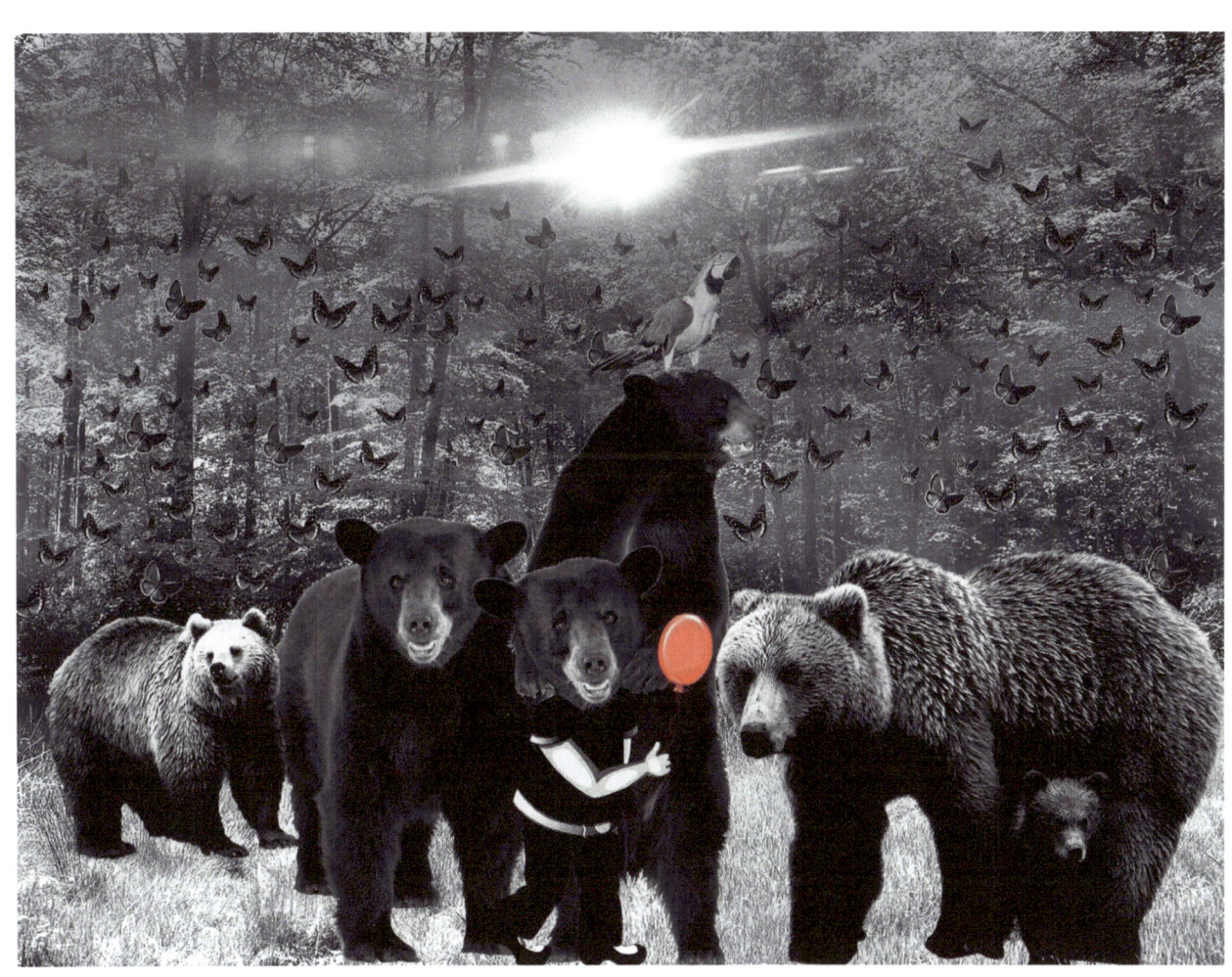

Then he rose up, and up, and up!

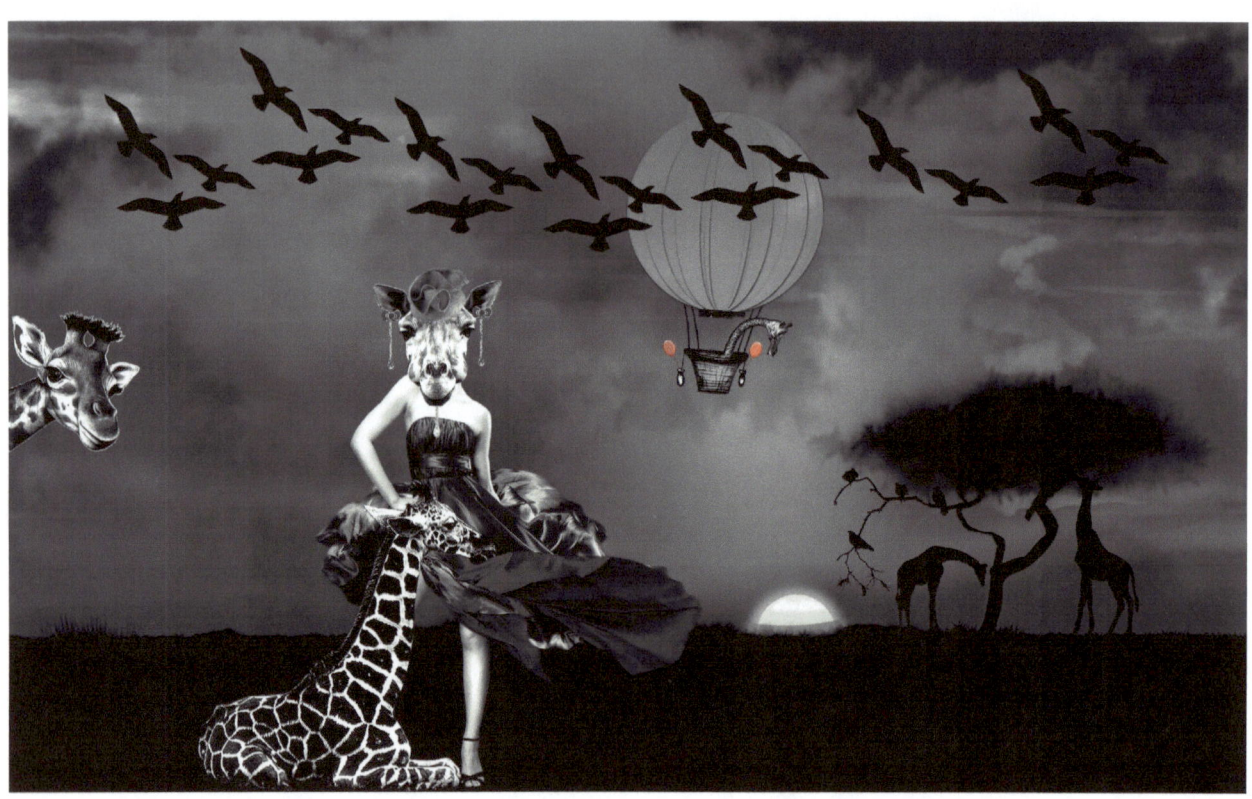

...and could see EVERYTHING!

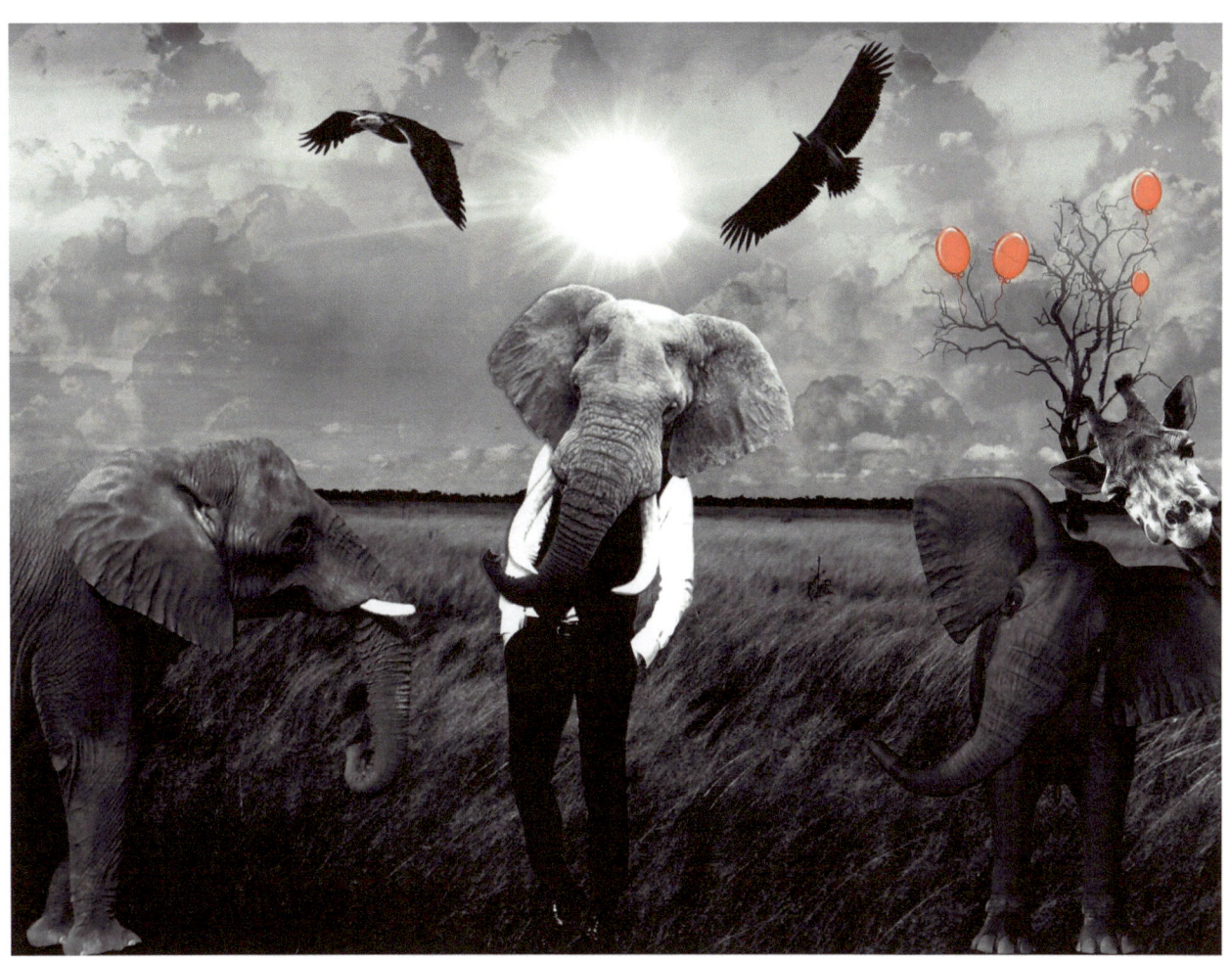

"My friend," he thought, "has done me good!"

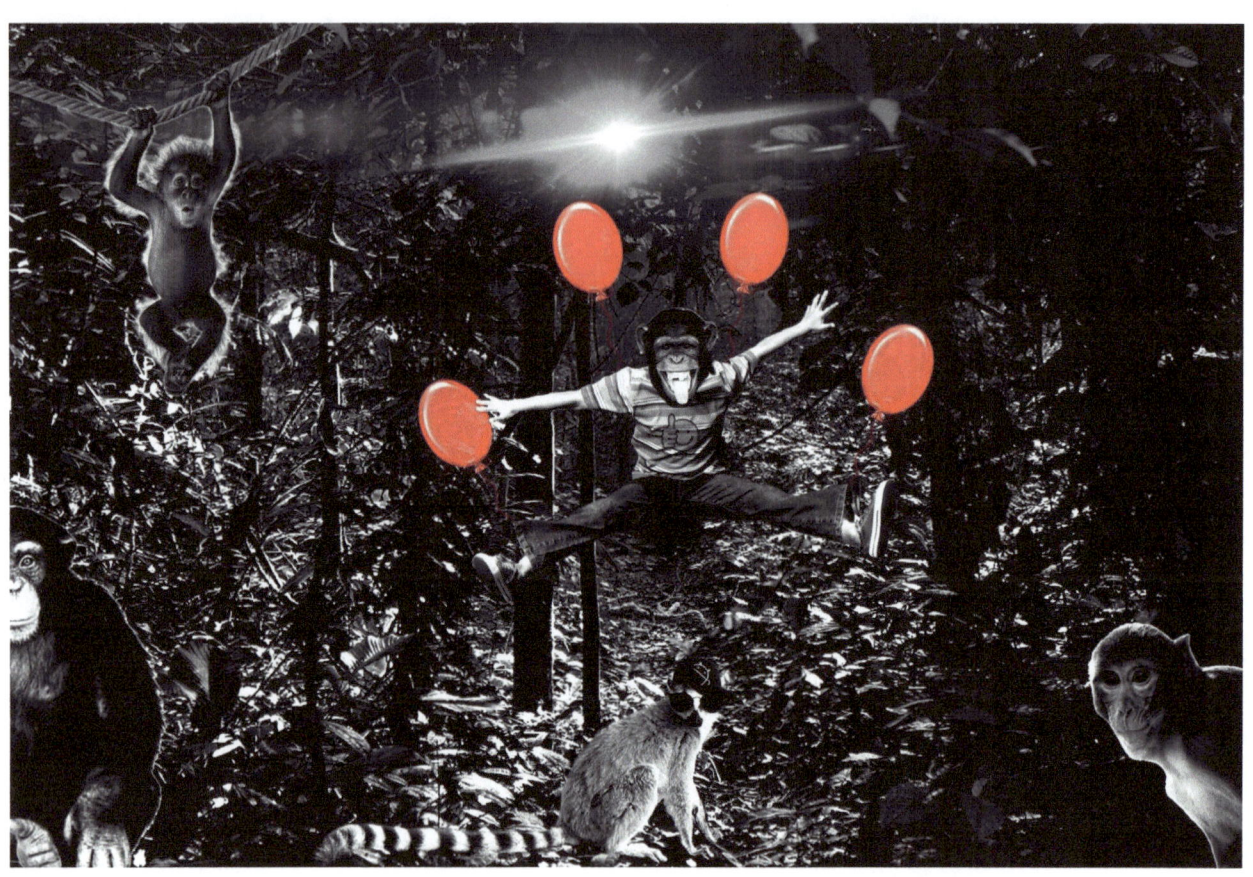

And now he understood!

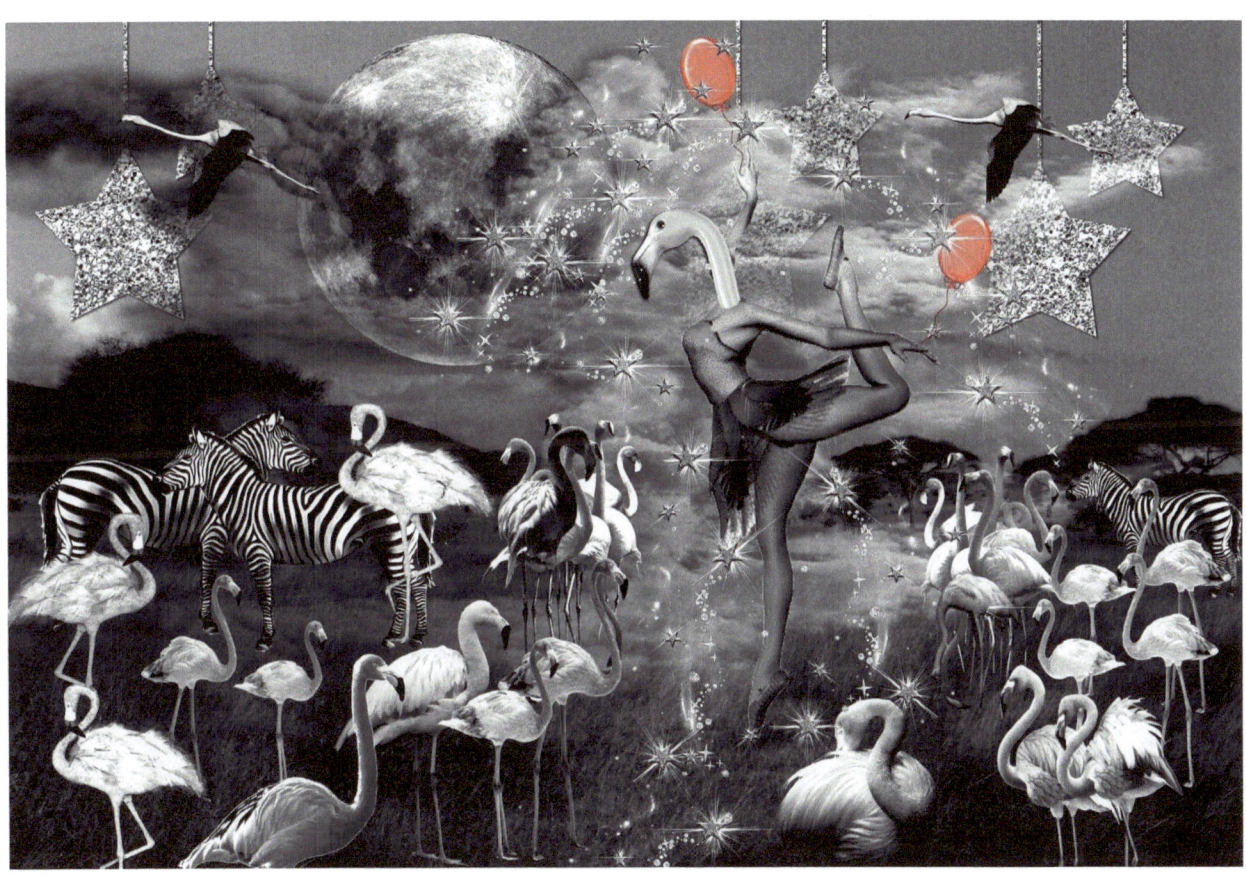

"Those who held me back

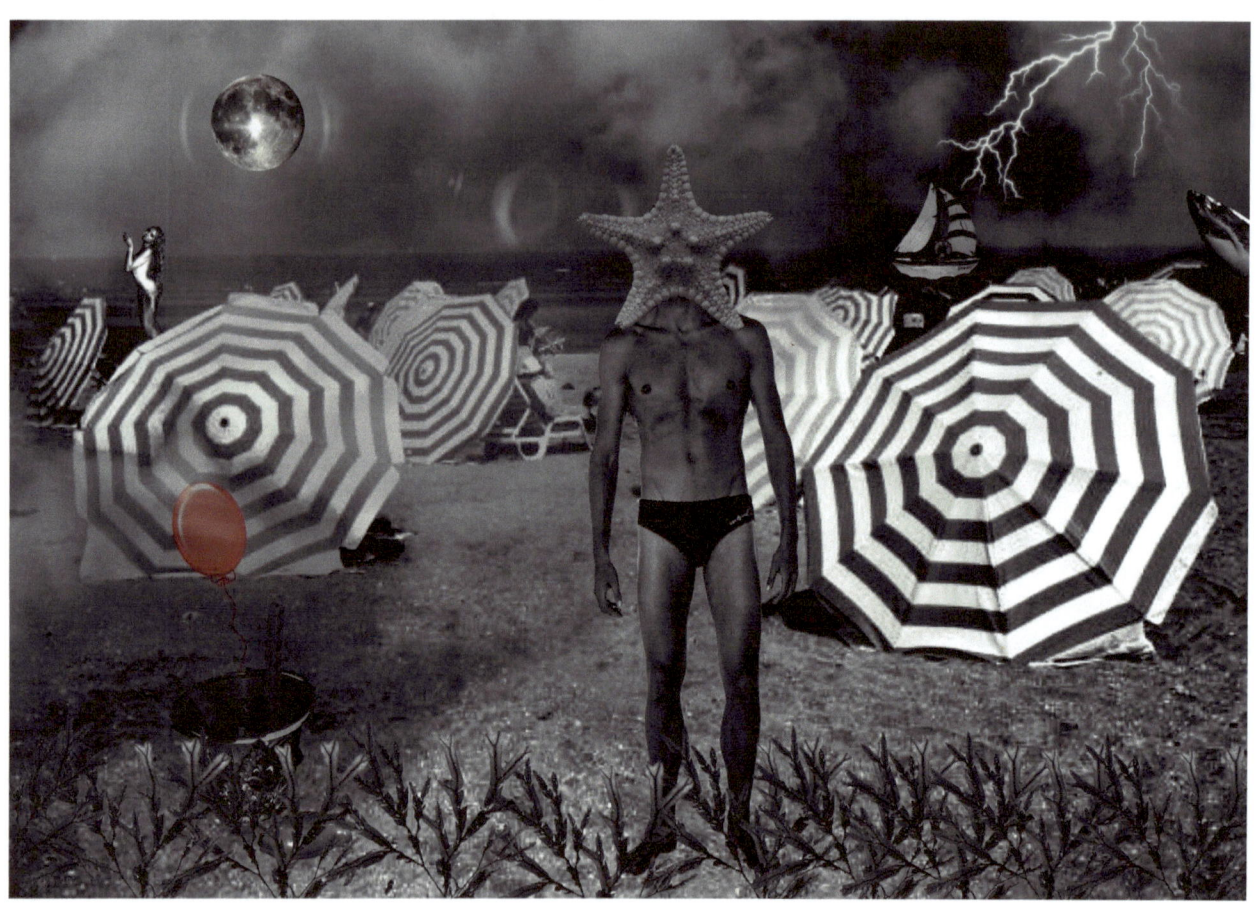

only sought for their own thrills.

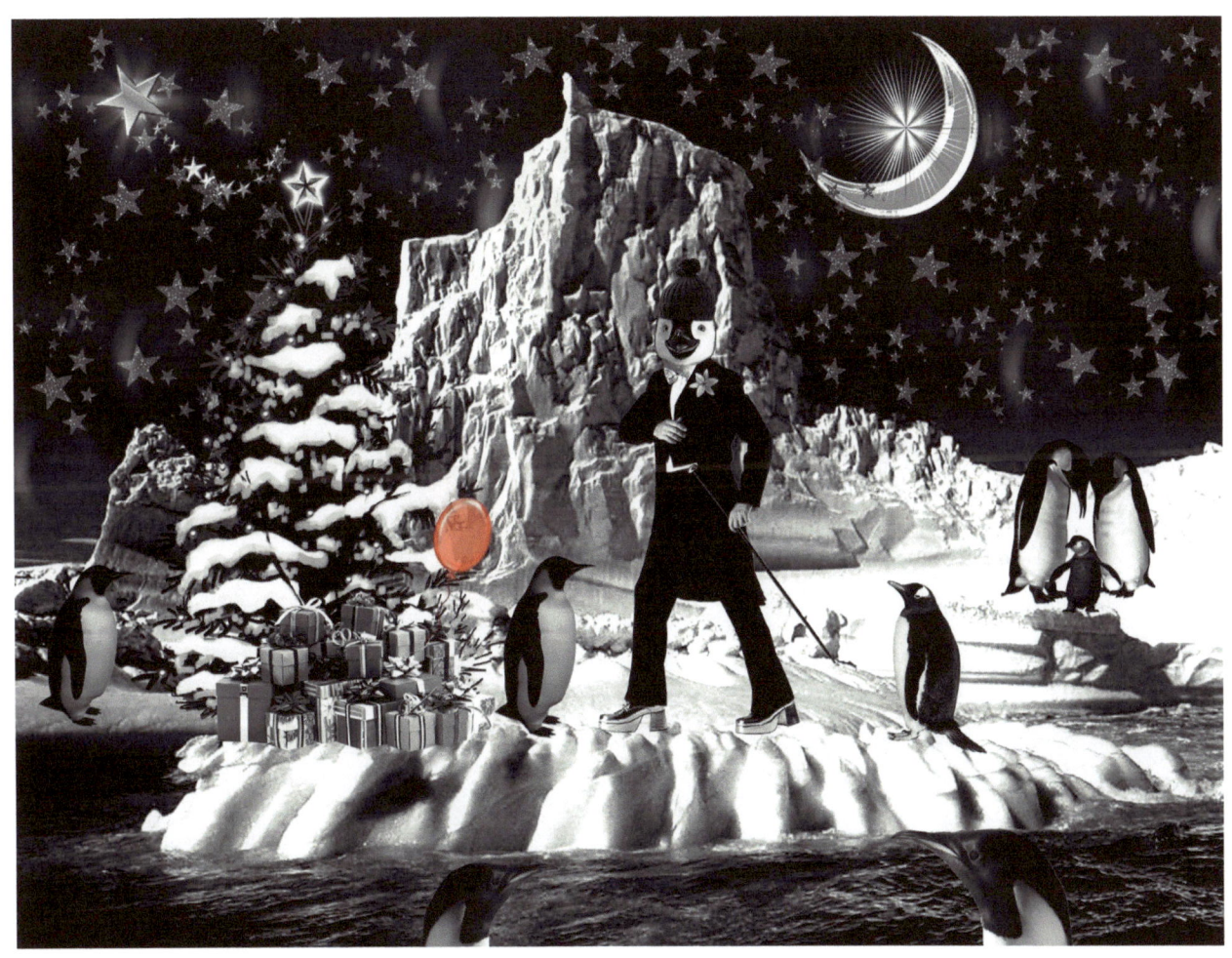

But the one who gave me wings to fly

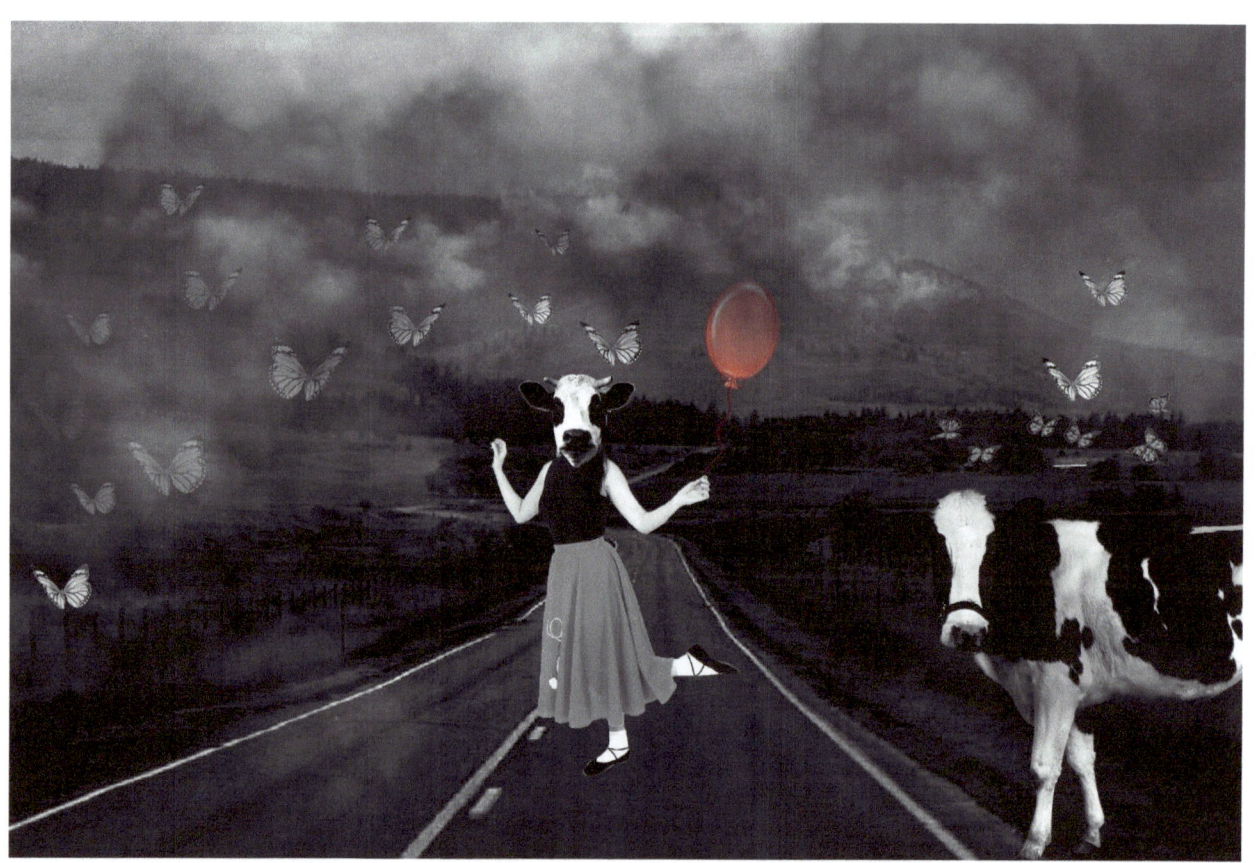

has given me free will!"

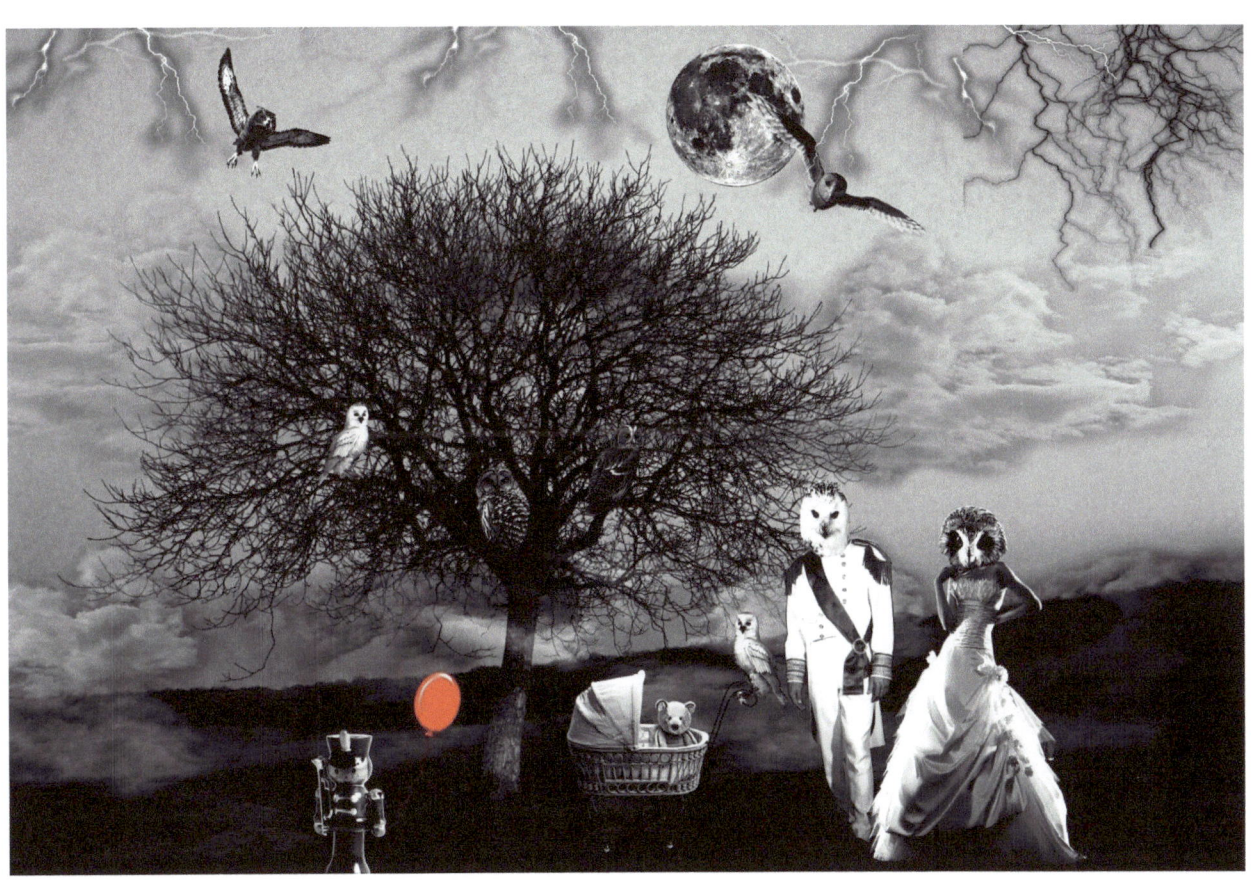

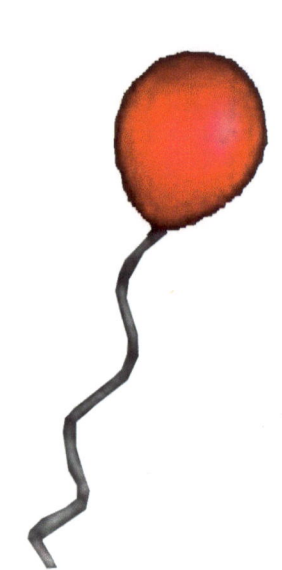

About the Photographer

Born in 1963, Jean-Luc Adde lives in Paris where he was a freelance photographer for 25 years, he first worked as a still photographer for film and television, and has directed since 2000 in a career of photojournalism. He's made numerous reports in different social circles such as the AIDS disease, schizophrenia, end of life, homelessness etc. His photos have been published in various journals and books.

Jean-Luc Adde is under contract with the International Agency reporters, Reporter Agency attached to various agencies such as Gamma and Sipa Press. He also outlined his personal work in New York, Venice, Istanbul, Brussels and Paris.

He has published ten books of photographs. For him, photography is a way of life. And what of the people who offer their perspectives on the purpose of life, and by their fight, their work, their will, their legacy for a moment shine as a light out of the shadows?

Jean-Luc ADDE wants to share with all who cross his path, during these fraternal times.

facebook.com/jeanluc.adde (Jean-Luc's personal profile)

jeanlucadde.com (Jean-Luc's official website)

Please LIKE and FOLLOW to see what's next!

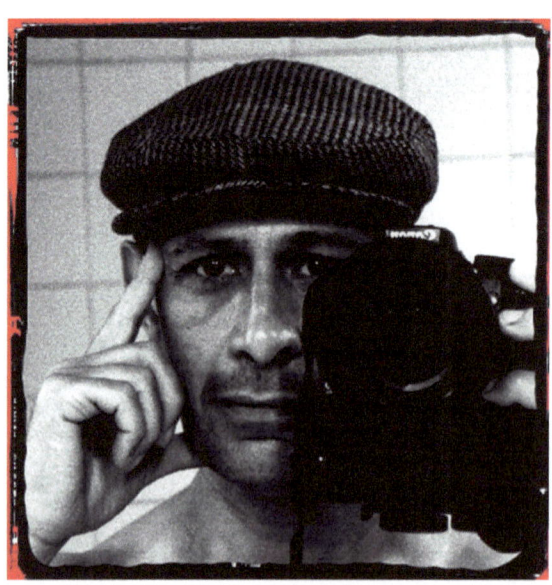

More books by Jean-Luc

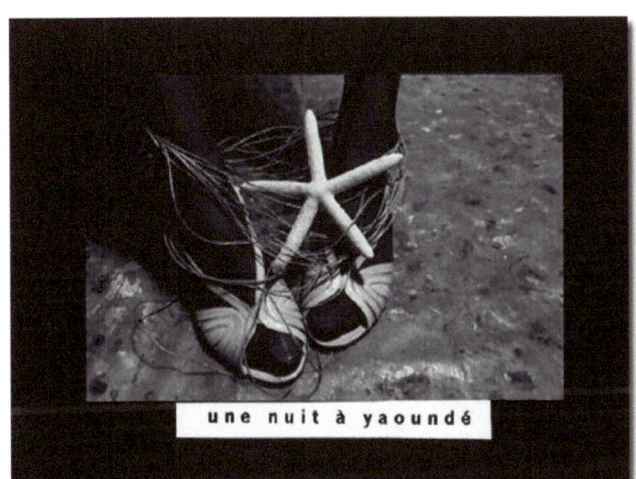

une nuit à yaoundé

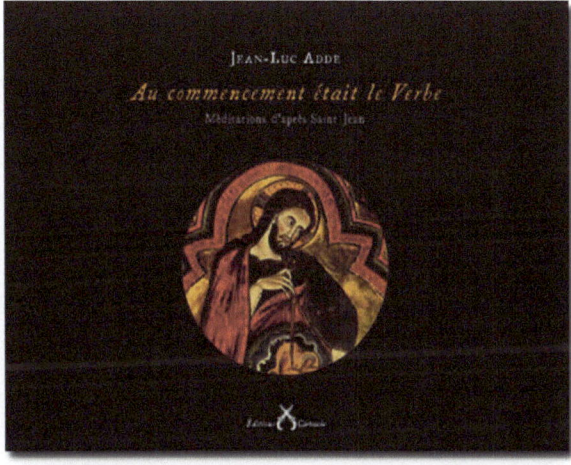

JEAN-LUC ADDE

Au commencement était le Verbe

Méditations d'après Saint Jean

Éditions Carmin

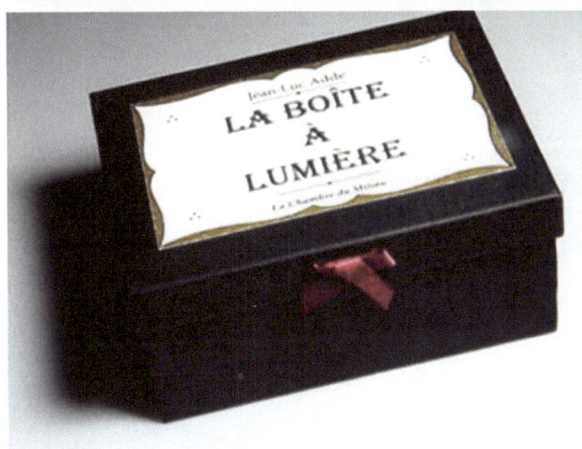

Jean-Luc Adde

LA BOÎTE
À
LUMIÈRE

La Chambre du Milieu

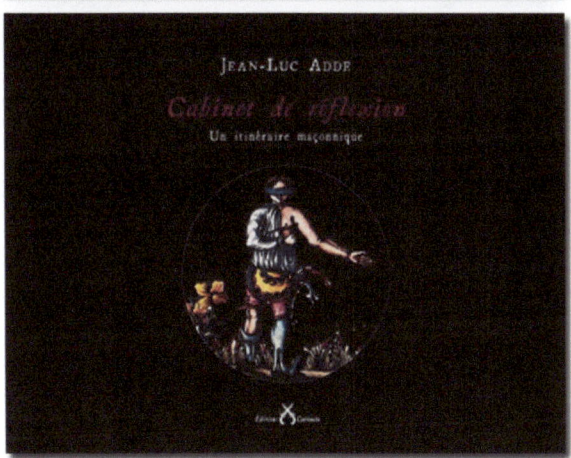

JEAN-LUC ADDE

Cabinet de réflexion

Un itinéraire maçonnique

Éditions Carmin

About the Author

Desiree began her artistic journey at a very young age. By the time she was 22 she had written hundreds of songs, released 7 studio albums and performed over 300 live shows in 11 states with various musical acts; all this while pursuing an art degree. After obtaining her degree, she left the music industry to focus on art, business and family. She owned and operated a small chain of extreme sports retail stores where she enjoyed creating best-selling products from her artwork, and licensed art to other companies and authors.

Her original award-winning art is now collected world-wide and she's written several novels, among them a best-selling series.

Today, Desiree lives an abundant and free life in the Ozark Mountains of NW Arkansas, in the heart of the mid-west, USA. With a passion for sustainability, green/off-grid technology, and organic gardening; Desiree is an activist for alternative living and participates in the civic duty of protecting the local environment for future generations to enjoy clean air, real food, and quality of life.

From her private multimedia studio, tucked away in the woods, she draws inspiration for writing, music and art from the beauty of nature and the tight-knit values of her local community... a community she helps build and maintain with constitutional values.

finkartstudio.com (for official archives, biography and galleries)

facebook.com/finkartstudio (for art/writing related news only)

facebook.com/desiree.finkbeiner (for the most active updates on all projects)

stores.ebay.com/Fink-Art-Studio (for original art and licensed products)

amazon.com/author/desireefinkbeiner (for books on Amazon)

Please LIKE and FOLLOW to see what's next!

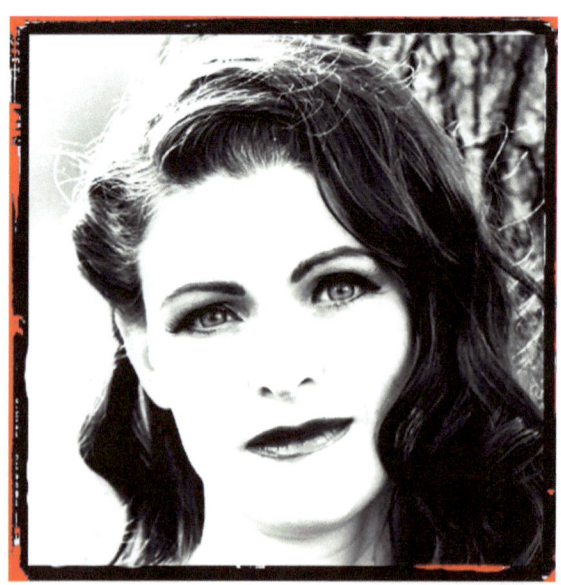

More books by Desiree

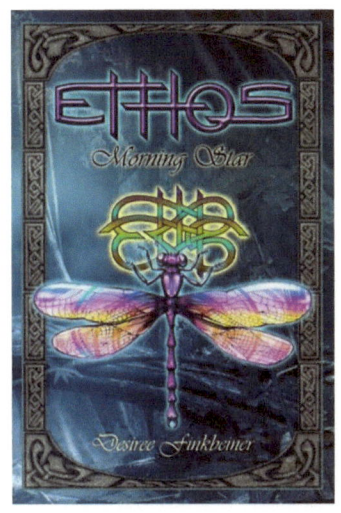 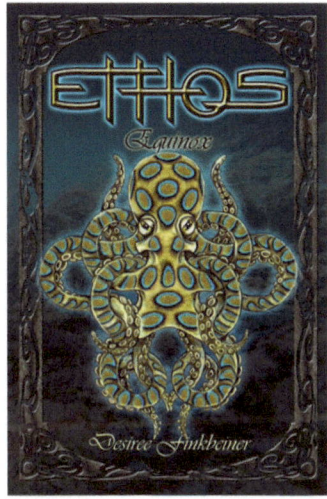 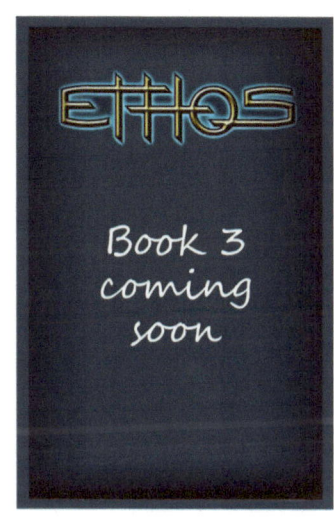

Best-Selling ETHOS Series. FIND IT ON AMAZON

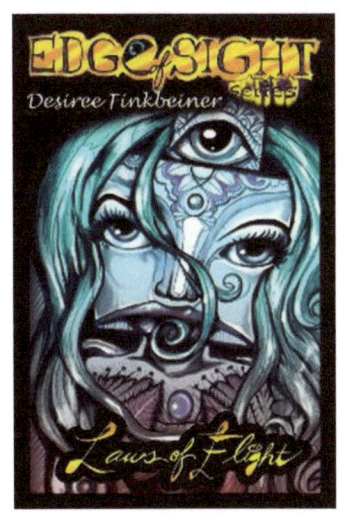

Many more works
in progress!
Follow Desiree on
Facebook for the
latest news!

Edge of Sight - Art & Poetry with NLP, on AMAZON

There is still room to dream...

Be free!

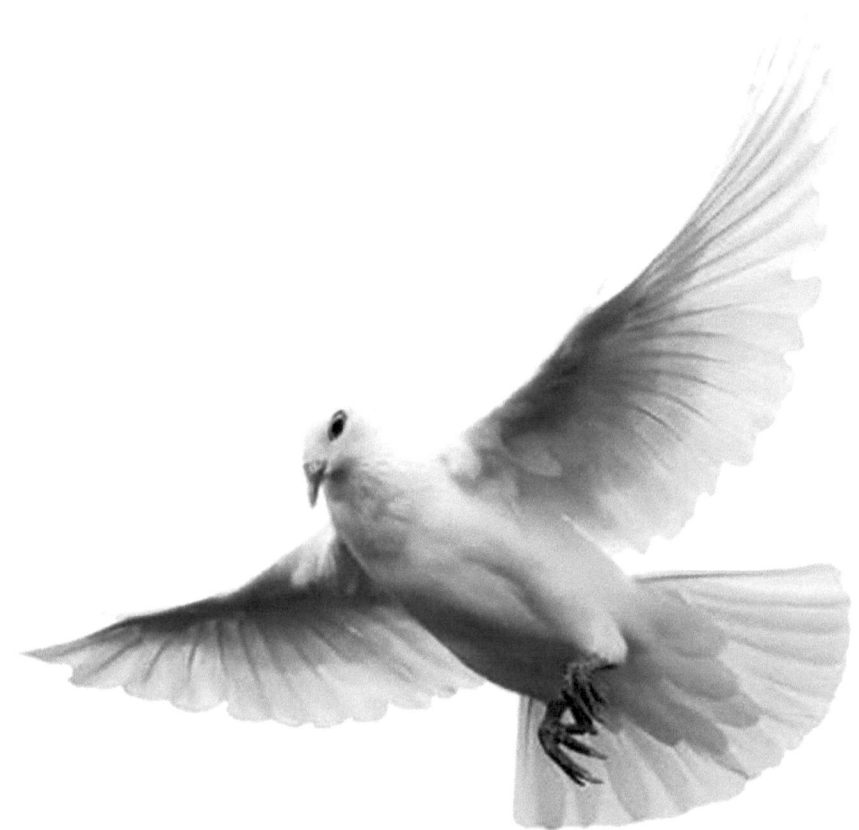

Little Red Balloon

A little red balloon
was tied onto a string.
But how he longed to soar the skies,
like birds do on their wings.

He felt trapped, to be tied up,
always fastened down.
In the hands of other folks,
he passed around the towns.

Though he saw some lights and streets,
some barns and stables too,
nothing could erase his dream
of having his own view.

A little girl noticed how he drooped,
and asked him why he frowned.
"Because, you see, I wish to be free
but here I am tied down."

"Then let me help you on your way!"
And she cut away his string...
Then he rose up, and up, and up!
...and could see EVERYTHING!

"My friend," he thought, "has done me good!"
And now he understood!

"Those who held me back
only sought for their own thrills.
But the one who gave me wings to fly
has given me free will!"

www.ingramcontent.com/pod-product-compliance
Lightning Source LLC
Chambersburg PA
CBHW040756200526

45159CB00026B/2821